I0616210

The Truth about Marriage

8 Principles for Sustaining a Christian Marriage

Chrissie Clay

Contents

1. Introduction and Prayer ... 1

2. The Truth about Marriage ... 3

3. Inviting God into the Bedroom ... 6

4. Prayer ... 10

5. Your Marriage is Under Warranty! ... 14

6. Pride ... 23

7. Submission ... 26

8. The Two Shall Be One Flesh ... 33

9. Your Marriage is a Battleground for Spiritual Warfare ... 36

10. What Now? ... 42

Introduction and Prayer

♥

Lord,

As this marriage You orchestrated continues, please always highlight my spouse's successes and capabilities. Please sow trust, security, and love into our marriage. Allow us to remember that we are blessed, and that this marriage is an honor in Your sight. Allow us to build each other up mentally, spiritually, emotionally, and physically.

When things are rough, allow us to seek You first. Allow us to forgive each other quickly. Grant us wisdom and knowledge to reconcile differences and resolve problems. Remind us that You've placed us in each other's lives for the rest of our lives.

In Jesus' name,

Amen

"Here is another thing you do. You cover the LORD's altar with tears, weeping and groaning because He pays no attention to your offerings and doesn't accept them with pleasure. You cry out, 'Why doesn't the LORD accept my worship?' I'll tell you why! Because the LORD witnessed the vows you and your wife made when you were young. But you have been unfaithful to her, though she remained your faithful partner, the wife of your marriage vows." Malachi 2:13-15.

The Truth about Marriage

The problem isn't that many couples don't invite God to their wedding. Think about it. People get married in a church, or have a servant of God perform the ceremony, meet at an altar, say a prayer, and even read a passage of scripture.

No, the problem isn't that many couples don't invite God to their wedding. It's that they leave Him there. They don't bring God into their marriage. They vow and commit before God and loved ones, and then turn their backs to the altar and leave God there.

The Bible says a three-braided cord is not easily broken (Ecclesiastes 4:9-12). Many couples have begun adding

3

this ritual to their ceremonies—some knowing the significance, others thinking it's cooler than lighting candles. They braid three cords: one symbolizing the man, one the woman, and one God. Yet, it's often not until everything is falling apart, or about to, that people remember that God is a part of their marriage. They want Him to step in and do something when it's going wrong but neglect the role He played when it was all right.

God is to be the core of all marriages. He is the creator of the institution of marriage after all (Genesis 2:21-25). He's not just to be called on when divorce is on the table. He's to be called on every day, in every circumstance, and for every situation. He is the sustainer of the marriage—not you or your spouse. In fact, you and your spouse are called to be obedient to God. Through your obedience, though it may not seem like it at first, God will fulfill wondrous works that only He can accomplish.

You need to get it together—regardless of what stage or year of marriage you're in. Jesus does not stop being the center of your life just because there's a band on your left hand. Being married increases territory, and therefore, increases more of what needs to be relinquished to God so that He may lord over your lives.

Many couples think the word "lord" is just a title that Jesus has. No. A lord is a master, an overseer, someone to whom people submit. When we submit our marriages to God, when we submit that amazing spouse that irks every single one of our nerves, we will truly be able to see His plans for our marital destinies.

Challenge:

Are you and your spouse guilty of "leaving God at the altar?" If so, what are some ways that you two can incorporate God into your marriage now? If you and your spouse didn't "leave God at the altar," then what areas of your marriage do you need to surrender to Him? What situations have you two left Him out of that He needs to be invited to?

Write down your answers and a plan to incorporate it in your marriage today. Afterward, pray for unity in your marriage, with you both acknowledging God as the center.

Scriptures:

- Ecclesiastes 4:9-12

- Malachi 2:13-15

Inviting God into the Bedroom

♥

Believe it or not, sex is also something that God created. Many Christians may feel like it's too dirty or taboo to talk to God about sex, but it shouldn't be. We talk to God about all of His other creations: the sky, the animals—why do we draw the line at sex? God Himself gave husbands and wives the command to "be fruitful and multiply" (Genesis 1:28). However, this doesn't mean that sex should only be engaged in for the sole purpose of reproducing. If that were the case, then as soon as people like Zechariah (John the Baptist's father; Luke 1:8-18) and Elkanah (Samuel's father; 1 Samuel 1) found out that their wives couldn't have children, they would've stopped having sex with them right then and there. No. Instead, we see husbands and wives engaging in the beautiful, sacred, God-ordained act whether reproducing is on the table or not.

So, what exactly does it mean to invite God into the bedroom? Whether or not you or your spouse have intimacy challenges, it doesn't hurt to ask God to come in and spend this time with you. I'm not saying you have to do a theatrical prayer. It could be as simple as, "Lord, please bless this experience we're about to encounter." You may even do this with or without your spouse's knowledge. The whole point is marital sex isn't a sin. It's not a "dirty" act that we need to leave God out of. If we're truly surrendering our marriage to God, then that includes sex. Allow Him to have full domain over the marriage.

Praying before sex could also prepare you emotionally, mentally, and spiritually. Ask God to clear your mind and all the pending tasks you need to complete. Ask God to help you be intentional and focus on your spouse. Ask God for it to be fun and enjoyable for both of you—regardless of how long or short it may be. Sex is covered in God's marriage plan.

Another benefit of allowing God to have a presence during your sexy time with your spouse is the revelation and discernment of what to do, what not to do, and the impact that doing something may have on your marriage bed. We all know the scripture about the marriage bed being undefiled (Hebrews 13:4), but what does that really mean? Yes, we know that other people should not be included during this time, but what other exclusions should there be? Praying allows you to ask God these questions. What's good for one person's marriage may not be beneficial to yours. Some things that you thought were okay may turn out to be damaging. Some things that you drew the line at God may say are ok.

Pray! Ask for wisdom, discernment, and an obedient heart to do whatever God tells you to. Therefore, resist the urge to feel dirty or to leave God waiting outside your bedroom door like your pet. Invite Him in. No harm can come from that.

Challenge:

Talk to your spouse about sex! Talk to each other and share a list with each other about some things you like, don't like, and want to try. Be respectful, understanding, and honest. If something makes you uncomfortable, then say it.

Don't be selfish! Be open to the other's ideas as long as it doesn't violate the will of God (anything that causes lust after another person is outside of the will of God). Bonus challenge: be vulnerable with your spouse. Explore each other's bodies.

Scriptures:

- Song of Solomon (Take your time and read all eight chapters. The language is very poetic, so use a version of the Bible that you understand best. Use a concordance and ask the Holy Spirit for help.)

- Hebrews 13:4

- 1 Corinthians 10:23

- 1 Corinthians 7:1-5

Prayer

Just like prayer is an important part of your personal relationship with Christ, it's also an important part of your marriage, of which Christ is a part. While many of us have our individual prayer times with Christ, we should also have—at a minimum—one time when we unite with our spouse and talk to Jesus, who is also in the marriage with us.

Naturally, this doesn't mean the only time that you should pray is when your spouse is present. Rather, you and your spouse should make time to pray together.

Some couples pray in the morning—either upon waking or before leaving home. Prayers during this time could include asking God for protection and wisdom throughout the day. It could be laying any questions, requests, or concerns that either one of you or both of you have at His feet. It could definitely be just thanking Him for all that He has done, including protecting your family through the night. It could be asking Him for grace to forgive and the discipline to continue to love each other unconditionally because the argument from last night is still fresh on everyone's minds.

Some couples pray at night or call each other during the day. Prayers like these could give God praise for His faithfulness throughout the day. It also allows the opportunity to clear the mind. Perhaps you and your spouse have a prayer list and use that to pray during your time with each other. Either way—it's acceptable in God's sight.

If one of you struggles with prayer, don't fret. Prayer, like everything else, gets better the more you do it. If you feel like you're the only one carrying the marital prayer life, then bring it to Jesus. He is the sustainer of both of your lives anyway. He's a part of the marriage, right? Let Him know how you feel if you're feeling overwhelmed by your spouse's lack of interest in prayer.

Prayer is essentially a conversation with God. Jesus gave us a model way to pray in Matthew 6. As this is a model prayer, the expectation is to use it as a skeleton or outline for our prayers—filling it in with details (the muscles).

For example:

Lord,

Thank You for being who You are: holy, magnificent, and wonderful. Thank You for seeing fit to bring us together. As we go out into the world today, we ask that You cover us and our family. We ask for protection, wisdom, guidance, love, patience, and self-control. Guard our hearts and minds and give us the desire and strength to detest anything that would bring harm to our marriage.

In Jesus' name,

Amen.

Your prayer could look similar to that or nothing like that at all. That's the beauty of prayer. It's personalized based on the personal relationship you have with your Father in Heaven.

There are unlimited possibilities when it comes to husbands and wives praying as one before the Creator who brought them together. You don't have to limit the prayer to once per day either. The Bible encourages us to pray without ceasing (1 Thessalonians 5:16-18, Philippians 4:6, Luke 18:1-8), so that alone should encourage us to not only seek God when we want to ask Him for something, but also when we want to give Him praise.

<u>Challenge:</u>

Make time to intentionally pray with your spouse. Have prayer points. Don't make this a one-time occurrence. Find a way to incorporate prayer daily.

<u>Scriptures:</u>

- Matthew 6:5-14

- Luke 18:1-8

- Ephesians 6:18

- Philippians 4:6

- 1 Thessalonians 5:16-18

Your Marriage is Under Warranty!

Stand in the Gap for Your Spouse

Warranty can be defined as a promise given to the buyer from the manufacturer that guarantees repair or replacement if needed. As Christians, we believe and know that God is the manufacturer of marriage. Within this institution exist certain elements, requirements, and parameters that we must abide by in order for the marriage to continue to work.

Some of these parameters include:

- Marriage existing between a male and a female (Genesis 5:2, Matthew 19:4).

- The male leaving his mother and father and cleaving unto his wife (Genesis 2:24, Matthew 19:5).

- The male and female becoming one physically and spiritually (Genesis 2:24, Matthew 19:6).

- The male and the female not inviting anyone else into their marriage (including sexually—whether that be in person, TV, book, phone, computer, etc.); God is the only third-party allowed in the marriage since He is a third of the three-braided cord mentioned earlier (Ecclesiastes 4:12, Hebrews 13:4, 1 Corinthians 7:2-6).

- Husbands and wives are to submit to each other (Ephesians 5:21).

- The husband is to be the head of the wife, and the head of the husband is God (Ephesians 5:23).

- The husband is to love his wife the same way that Christ loves the church and gave Himself as a sacrifice for her. In other words, the same way Christ loves us and goes to war for us is the same expectation that husbands are to strive to achieve

(Ephesians 5:25-27; 1 Peter 3:7).

- Husbands are to love their wives the same way they love themselves (Ephesians 5:28-30, 33; 1 Peter 3:7).

- Wives are to respect and honor their husbands. The same way wives respect and honor Christ is the same way wives are to respect and honor their husbands. If you wouldn't talk back to Christ, don't do it to your husband. If you wouldn't curse Christ out, then don't do it to your husband (Ephesians 5:22, 24; 1 Peter 3:1-2)

- Let no one separate the marriage. The Bible says, "What God has joined together, let no man put asunder." Matthew 19:6. Emphasis on the fact that this is talking about a union created by God.

Remember: these are just some of the instructions that the Manufacturer put in place for marriages to run as effectively as possible. So, how's the marriage under warranty? A warranty must be used, or issued, or requested when something goes wrong. When something needs to be fixed, updated, readjusted, or recalled, the first question asked is, "Do you have a warranty?"

Some issues that require couples to use their warranty include:

- One or both of the spouses start lying.

- One or both of the spouses become deceptive and/or manipulative.

- Onc or both of the spouses turn their back(s) on Christ.

- One or both of the spouses start cheating, lusting, or watching pornography.

- One or both of the spouses begin doing questionable activities (stealing, gambling foolishly, becoming addicted to substances, etc.).

- One or both of the spouses become disrespectful towards the other.

- Anything that violates the parameters that were set by the Manufacturer is when the warranty has to be used.

**Reminder: This only applies to the God-created marriages. A lot of people run off and get married, claiming, "God told me to, so it's okay," or "God didn't stop me from getting married, so He approves of it." These marriages are not under warranty because God never intended for you to be with that person.

Once the marriage "vehicle" starts acting up, starts getting its wear and tear, and things start falling out of place, you aren't to run to the "quick-fix mechanic" down the road. The "quick-fix mechanic" in this analogy is a divorce lawyer, or a side piece, or drugs or alcohol, or going back home to your parents' house, or pretending to be married while y'all sleep in two different rooms with two different lives. According to your warranty, you're supposed to bring the marriage back to the Manufacturer because at the end of the day, He is the only one who can fix what went wrong.

Think about instances when cars are recalled. The manufacturer doesn't pull up to your house, ring your doorbell, and say, "We're taking this car." The same way you're expected to take your car to the dealership is the same way you're expected to take your marriage to God. Take your marriage to the altar, take your marriage to the war room, take your marriage to the prayer closet, and give it to the Manufacturer and say, "This needs to be fixed."

The beautiful thing about cars is that it only takes one person to drive it for it to work. So even if your God-given spouse is ready to call it quits, it only takes one of you to bring the marriage back to God and say, "I need help. It's not just two of us in this marriage; it's all *three* of us! You were at that altar when we got married. You were there when we got engaged. You were there when we started dating. It was You that we made our vows to. It's You that we pray to. It's You that we dedicated these rings to, and our marriage to, and our relationship to, God. So, I need you to step in, and I need you to activate this warranty on this marriage because we said, 'until death do us part,' and Lord, neither one of us is dead. So, this lifelong institution should still be covered under this lifelong warranty.

How does the Manufacturer fix the marriage? God's ways aren't our ways, nor are His thoughts our thoughts. I can't tell you to follow points 1-6, and then your marriage will be restored. The truth of the matter is we serve a very creative, all-knowing God. Therefore, the way He applies the warranty to my marriage may not be the same way He applies the warranty to your marriage. The beautiful thing about marriage is what's wrong with mine may not be what's wrong with yours, but even if it is the same problem, the solution could be very different.

The first thing God may tell you to do is to break the covenant with what's destroying your marriage. Somewhere along the line, lust was introduced into the marriage; gambling debt and addiction to drugs and alcohol were introduced into the marriage. Somewhere along the line, selfishness and narcissism were introduced into the marriage. Somewhere along the line pridefulness was introduced into marriage, and you didn't want to listen to your spouse because you believed you knew it all. God is going to tell you to get back to living inside of the parameters He established. Ask for forgiveness. Repent. Ask God to bring you back inside the parameters of His protection because once you step out of the boundaries that God created, you now become susceptible to the consequences of the things you left Him for.

God may have you do more than just this one step, but the important thing to remember is to not become dismayed. Be of good cheer and of good heart. Your marriage is covered under the blood of Jesus Christ. You don't have to wait until your marriage vehicle breaks down in order to bring it to the Mechanic. Go in for service checks! Go in for an oil change! Having godly counsel is nothing to be ashamed of. Have those hard conversations. Listen even when it feels like you're being ridiculed. Talk and make changes as needed.

Remember to always invite God to spend time with y'all. Invite Him into every aspect of your marriage—whether y'all are just going on a walk, whether y'all are going out on a date, or whether y'all are coming home to make love—invite God. That's how you maintain the marriage. This doesn't mean you won't have any problems. We are flawed humans living in a flawed world, after all. However, when the problems arise, you know that they won't shake you too hard. You know it won't lead to your alternator going out, it won't lead to your battery dying—all it would lead to is a tune-up.

Challenge:

Write and discuss ways/areas that you and your spouse have been neglectful. Talk about and come up with a plan for strengthening the weak areas (this may not be completed in one sitting). Get rid of anything that is detrimental to your marriage or anything that you've allowed into your marriage that was outside of God's original marriage blueprint. Pray and ask God to reveal what needs to be improved. Fight for your marriage!

<u>Scriptures:</u>

- Song of Solomon 2:15

- 1 Corinthians 7:12-16

- Ephesians 5:21-33

- 1 Peter 3:1-2, 7

Pride

What gets bruised the most in marriage isn't your heart—it's your pride. Your ego. Your desire to not back down despite knowing that winning the argument, or disagreement, if you prefer a softer synonym, will emotionally wound your spouse and/or your marriage. Your thinking of, "Yeah, I see your point, but I see my point too, and this time I'm going to choose my point over yours." No, I'm not talking about a physically, verbally or emotionally abusive marriage. I'm talking about a pride-driven marriage.

Humility is the opposite of pride. Humility says, "Even though I know I'm right, I'm going to let you have it." Maybe it's not humility that's the opposite of pride. Perhaps it's love. Love says, "I see the trap that's been laid in front of us. We're meant to argue and spend all night tossing and turning so we won't go to sleep—giving the devil a foothold." Love says, "I see that trap, but I won't fall into it. I'm also not going to let you fall into it, so before we both say something we'll regret later, I'll leave this conversation. I'll change my response. I have the retort that will humble you, but I love you, I love our marriage, I love God, and I honor the commitment I made before Him too much to let my pride get in the way."

Pride is the killer of love. Pride says, "I honor myself and what I think or feel above you or the situation at hand." Pride says, "I'm going to do it my way, and either you're going to get on board, or you're going to go through it on your own." Pride is the thing that whispers in your ear and says, "Remember when you were single? You didn't have anyone to answer to. You could do stuff without consulting anyone. Are you just going to let this person tell you what you've been doing all your life is wrong?"

Pride is the killer of marriages. Pride tells you not to apologize first because you didn't start it. Because your point was valid. Because you always apologize first. Because what you said made more sense. Because you've been a Christian longer. Pride goes against everything Jesus taught. Jesus was compassionate, forgiving, and humble.

The antithesis of petty. You can't have the love of Christ and the pride of Satan in you at the same time.

Overcome pride with love. Have self-control. Be gentle. Be kind. Have joy. Be peaceful. Be faithful to your commitment to the Lord and to your spouse. Forgive as quickly as you want God to forgive you. Love as deeply as God has loved you and commanded you to do. Cast out every shadow of pride from your marriage, your home, and your lives. Pray. Remember Romans 12:2, 9-21.

Challenge:

What are you prideful about? What are some things you don't back down from even when you know you're wrong? Make a list. Repent and ask God for forgiveness. Then ask God to give you strength (because humility takes strength) and direction to live a humble life.

Scriptures:

- Galatians 5:16-26

- Proverbs 16:18

- Proverbs 11:2

Submission

There's such a negative stigma around the word "submission," especially when it comes to Christian marriages. Everyone always says, "Wives need to submit to their husbands," but this is only half true. The reality is that the Bible commands husbands and wives to submit to each other.

Paul gave us twelve verses in Ephesians 5, instructing us on how husbands and wives are to interact with one another. Verses 22 and 23 say, "For wives, this means submit to your husbands as to the Lord. For a husband is the head of his wife as Christ is the head of the church..." A lot of people start and stop right here, ignoring verse 21 which says, "And further submit to one another out of reverence for Christ." They fail to acknowledge that verse 21 sets the tone for the verses that follow. Verse 21 is Paul's command to the couple as a whole, while verses 22-24 are Paul's command to the wives, and verses 25-30 are Paul's command to the husbands. They're both required to submit, but the requirements of the submission differ.

Submission to one another becomes easier when you realize that you're to submit to God first. If you're submitted to God, then you'll keep the peace in your house and not get the last word because you submit to God's scriptures that warn against careless talk and approve of words of encouragement.

Most women find it hard to wholly submit to their husbands for a variety of reasons. Reasons range from not trusting their husbands will lead correctly to being afraid of giving up their independence. As a young adult, I often heard my mother say, "Do not enter into marriage lightly." There are serious ramifications for entering into marriage rashly; one of them, for women, includes submitting to a man whom you may deem unfit to lead you. But God is merciful, and if your husband is the spouse God destined you to be with, then with your fervent prayers, God can lead and mold your husband into who he needs to be. Submitting to your husband means submitting to him the way the church submits to Christ, but it doesn't mean committing crimes or sin with your husband. God gives us free access to wisdom, and the Holy Spirit is forever ready to provide discernment; thus, you will have the opportunity to know when you should tell your husband to reconsider a decision or action.

Submitting doesn't always mean completely losing yourself (though as you and your husband mesh into one flesh, and as God continually edifies you, the person you were when you got married may slowly evaporate anyway). It also isn't being so obsessed with your husband that he becomes your idol. There is a healthy level of submission that God requires of His daughters. It doesn't resemble Sarah, who went against God's word and took reproducing into her own hands, but it resembles Mary, who submitted to her husband and moved when he said it was time to move, though she was carrying the Messiah. Our obedience to God by submitting to our husbands displays our trust in God and yields His rewards. As seen when Sarah told Abraham to sleep and reproduce with Hagar, wives acting on their own and outside the will of God will create unnecessary predicaments (read what happened to Hagar and her son in Genesis if you don't believe me).

Submission may not be easy, especially when you're more spiritually mature than your husband. You may ask, "Why do I have to submit when he can't even pray properly or interpret scripture accurately?" The simple answer: because you're commanded to. Your husband will develop a prayer life by watching and listening to you. Your husband will learn about scripture when you sit down with him and discuss it together. Your husband can be a better spiritual leader when you remember that God has to be the one to lead him; you're just a helping hand. Salvation comes through Christ, not you, Mrs.

Husbands, believe it or not, you must submit too. To start, you must submit to God no matter what. If you aren't submitting to God, you're out of order. If God is telling you to listen to what your wife says, and you ignore it for any reason, you're out of order with God. The same way women trust God to give them a husband to lead them according to His will is the same way you have to trust that God gave you a wife who will support and encourage you wherever and through whatever God has in store. Somewhere in history the belief of "what the man says goes," came about and has been used to demand unquestioning submission from wives to husbands. However, 1 Peter 3 tells husbands to consider wives as their equal partners because wives are equal heirs with them in the Kingdom of Heaven. Peter also cautions husbands to treat their wives as they should so that their prayers won't be hindered or ineffective. In short, you can't nullify or ignore what your wife says because she's a woman, nor can you treat her carelessly since she is a daughter of God.

Husbands should love their wives to the extent that Christ loves the church. Christ loves His bride to the point of consecrating her. He cleaned her and made sure she had no faults so that He could present her to Himself. Christ even died for his bride. That's how devoted and loving husbands are called to be. Does that mean telling your wife yes to everything she wants? Of course not. If your wife is materialistic, feeding into her habits won't keep her on the straight and narrow road. Pray for her to have wisdom and contentment with whatever situation God has placed you two in. Pray for your wife to be resourceful like the Proverbs 31 woman so that your wife doesn't mismanage your household or funds. If anything in her needs to be changed or altered, don't make fun of her—encourage her to make the changes. *Join* her on the journey to making those changes. The way you love your wife shows how much you love yourself.

Your submission to your wife also requires you to leave the comfort of home. Your mom may be your number one girl, but once you're married, your wife becomes the number one woman in your life. Your mother should not dictate what goes on in your marriage or household; it doesn't matter how upset she gets. Your wife is your queen and the co-ruler of your home. If you weren't ready for that level of commitment, you shouldn't have gotten married, and if you're not married but reading this, don't get married if you don't agree with this statement. The Bible repeatedly says that "A man leaves his father and mother and is joined to his wife, and the two are united into one." If you bring your momma, your father, and your homeboys (or homegirls), you just created a group chat—not a union. You can't be a leader while simultaneously taking orders from your family or friends. God is the only one you should be taking orders from. God may *choose* to speak to you through family, friends, or your pastor, but He will also speak to you directly. After all, you're the one who's supposed to cover His daughter.

Love your wife the way Christ loved the church. Love your wife as you love yourself.

Challenge:

How well do you two do with submitting to one another? Where do you fall short? Read Ephesians 5:21-33 and 1 Peter 3:1-7. Discuss your answers to the above questions and discuss your thoughts on the two scriptures. Pray for the ability and desire to submit to one another as God has commanded. This may take work, so keep in mind that results may not happen overnight. Remember, this isn't an opportunity to point out where one falls short, but to encourage one another to live in obedience to God's will.

Scriptures:

- Ephesians 5:21-23 (feel free to read the whole chapter if need be)

- 1 Peter 3:1-7 (feel free to start from chapter 4, verse 13)

The Two Shall Be One Flesh

Sure, it sounds cute and sweet, but what does it really mean? Marriage is about the colliding of two forces who more than likely come from different backgrounds but have been joined together by an omniscient God who declared that the two are better as one. However, combining two independent variables into a single place and requiring them to function as one can be chaotic. This union is comparable to two colors that must be mixed, red and white, for example. Both are independent variables that can sustain themselves and behave as they like. When combined, however, the two colors make pink. Pink is a new color, a new foundation, and a new variable that otherwise would not exist if red and white never joined. *That's* what two becoming one is. There has to be the right amount of white so that it doesn't dilute the red, and there has to be the right amount of red so that it doesn't overpower the white.

Hopefully by now it is clear that we're not just speaking about colors. Two becoming one is more than just sex, last names, and a house. Becoming one is compromise; it's a give and take, and this exchange isn't always fifty-fifty. I dare say marriage is rarely ever fifty-fifty. Sometimes you may have to give seventy percent, whereas other times you may only have thirty percent to offer. Times may exist when you need more than fifty percent from your spouse, whereas other times you're satisfied with twenty-five. Your marriage can be steadfast while also being malleable (yes, it's a paradox). Marriage wasn't created to be stagnant, but to grow and evolve with you and your spouse as the two of you grow and evolve through the various seasons God leads you through. Remember, becoming one is more than physical. It's two beings uniting to form a brand new one. Picture it like Power Rangers' Zords. Individually, they have the ability to fight and hold their own, but it's not until they combine into the Megazord that they reach their full potential.

Challenge:

List 3-4 tasks that you and your spouse have different views on. On one occasion, complete the task the husband's way. On another occasion, complete it the wife's way. Be non-judgmental and unbiased; be open to the new experience(s). Afterward, share thoughts, and see if there's a way to compromise, or if one person's way is more beneficial than the other.

Scriptures:

- Genesis 2:18-25

- Ecclesiastes 4:9-12

- Matthew 19:3-6

- Ephesians 5:31-33

Your Marriage is a Battleground for Spiritual Warfare

♥

I've been there too! The argument with your spouse that seems to have come out of nowhere. The words they said that triggered you to act a certain way because you still have unresolved trauma. The way that they did something that they usually always do, but today it's the last straw because you just can't take it anymore. Yes! Warfare. And war is... ugly.

Before we dive in, we must understand that not every argument is an attack from the enemy. Sometimes the argument is because one of us didn't follow directions properly, or one of us didn't communicate as well as we should have. Sometimes we just do things that we know get on our spouse's nerves, but we assume that today is the day it won't bother them. No, things like these require deliverance and self-control. We are humans, and we will make mistakes, but our spouses shouldn't have to religiously remind us why they don't like when we do certain things.

This topic is about the spiritual attacks that we have no control over. It's about the foxes that the women in Song of Solomon told us to protect our gardens against. It's about having a season where everything is fine, and before you know it, you're in a season of " Why do I even talk to you?" Yeah, *that* spiritual warfare.

The Bible says that the enemy comes to steal, kill, and destroy. Steal the pleasures of marriage, kill the relationship between the two in the marriage, and destroy the unity of the marriage. Marriage is a union created by God. A key synonym of union is unity. You and your spouse are one. Satan's goal for your marriage is simple: divide and conquer. Division places you out of God's blueprint, so even when your spouse is the most annoying creature on the planet, you two must remain one.

This doesn't mean that there won't be times when you all have to take a few moments of silence or take a break from the conversation. But it does mean that you can't go to bed angry. It does mean you can't be petty or plot for revenge. It does mean you have to forgive, even if they have yet to apologize. Conflict resolution is different from situation to situation and couple to couple. However, Jesus is the peacemaker, so with His guidance and wisdom, you can make it through any attack. The outcome may be different than expected, but if it is in God's will, ask Him for peace to accept it and move on.

Song of Solomon 2:15 says, "Catch all the foxes, those little foxes, before they ruin the vineyard of love, for the grapevines are blossoming!" At first glance, it may seem as though the singer wants you to protect your physical vineyard from physical foxes. While this is good advice, remember that this book is filled with symbolism and other figurative language. The garden/ vineyard is used as an extended metaphor, comparing marriage to the vineyard that must be protected from "little foxes." Those foxes are the little spats y'all get into with no hope for resolution. Those foxes are the items swept under the rug instead of being brought to the light. Those foxes are people who are so involved in your marriage that you don't make a move without telling them first. Those foxes are the rough edges you refuse to iron out—the difficult conversations that you'd rather not have.

Allowing these foxes to run around gives the enemy access to plant his attacks against you. Catch them. The verse's only instruction is to catch them, but I dare you to go a step further. After catching them, launch those foxes out of your garden—out of your marriage. As it was previously mentioned, there is only enough room in your marriage for three beings—you, your spouse, and God. Can God use other people to speak to you and help you with marriage? Of course. But the issue is when that third person (or thing) becomes the fourth being in your marriage.

The scriptures tell us that earthly marriages are a representation of our marriage to Christ. Just like we engage in daily battles with the enemy to maintain our walk with the Lord, is the same way our marriage will be attacked so that we won't desire to stay together anymore.

Tips for Combatting this Warfare:
- **Pray!** Whether it's together, individually, or you have to call someone to do it—pray.

- **Acknowledge that it is spiritual warfare.** If there seems to be no explanation for the discordance happening, seek God and confirm that this is spiritual warfare. (Please keep in mind that all trials don't come from the enemy. Remember Job's plight. Some storms may be sent to see how well you can whether them. Build your house upon the Rock.)

- **If it gets too heated, take a break.** No, I'm not talking about in your marriage, or someone going to a hotel. I'm talking about giving the conversation or disagreement a break. I'm talking about a moment to gather yourself—to attempt to see it from the other's perspective. A break with the understanding that the topic will have to be revisited to be resolved. You can forgive each other to not go to bed angry but agree to revisit the topic the following day.

Challenge:

Today's challenge is about endurance and patience through teamwork. Complete a puzzle, beat an escape room, build a house of cards, or play a video like *It Takes*

Two or *Split Fiction*. Whatever activity you choose, you and your spouse must complete it together, while being patient with and not giving up on each other.

Scriptures:

- Isaiah 54:17

- Romans 12:21

- 2 Corinthians 10:3-6

- Ephesians 4:2-3

- Ephesians 6:10-18

- James 4:7

What Now?

♥

Thank you for taking the time to read these principles. Whether you're happily married, going through a hard time in your marriage, or engaged and looking for a good foundation, I pray that the Lord blesses and enriches your union. Keep in mind that this isn't a "fix all," as marriages, like our relationships with Christ, are individually personalized. That said, these principles are beneficial biblical truths. Feel free to journal as you read. Ask for God to reveal specific truths to you and your spouse. Reread this as needed. Feel free to connect with me:

Amazon: ChrissieClay Author Page

Facebook: Chrissie Clay - Author

Instagram: Chrissie_Clay

TikTok: Chrissie.Clay